D0471601

Plotting Points and Position

09/2006   Jfund   26⁰⁰

© Aladdin Books Ltd 1998
Produced by
Aladdin Books Ltd
28 Percy Street
London W1P OLD

First published in
the United States
in 1998 by
Copper Beech Books,
an imprint of
The Millbrook Press
2 Old New Milford Road
Brookfield, Connecticut 06804

Project Editor: Sally Hewitt
Editor: Liz White
Design: David West Children's Book Design
Designer: Simon Morse
Photography: Roger Vlitos
Illustrator: Tony Kenyon

Printed in Belgium
All rights reserved
5 4 3 2 1

**Library of Congress
Cataloging-in-Publication Data**
King, Andrew, 1961-
Plotting points and position / by Andrew King ;
illustrated by Tony Kenyon.
p. cm. — (Math for fun)
Includes index.
Summary: Uses games and projects to introduce the concepts of
coordinates and angles to find location and position.
ISBN 0-7613-0852-0 (lib. bdg.).
— ISBN 0-7613-0746-X (pbk.)
1. Graphic methods—Juvenile literature.
2. Coordinates—Juvenile literature.
3. Angle—Juvenile literature.
[1. Graphic methods. 2. Coordinates. 3. Angle.]
I. Kenyon, Tony, ill. II. Title.
III. Series: King, Andrew, 1961-
Math for fun.
QA90.K525 1998   98-18034
516.16—dc21   CIP AC

MATH *for fun*

Plotting Points and Position

Andrew King

Copper Beech Books
Brookfield, Connecticut

CONTENTS

INTRODUCTION

Explorers use coordinates to plot the position of their discoveries. Astronomers use angles to pinpoint the position of stars and to plan journeys into space. You can find hidden treasure, get through mazes, and make fascinating patterns easily when you know about coordinates, angles, and symmetry.

Try out the amazing activities, fun games, and practical projects in this book and you can have fun learning about plotting points and position.

● Follow the STEP-BY-STEP INSTRUCTIONS to help you with the activities.

● Use the HELPFUL HINTS for clues about the experiments and games.

● Look at MORE IDEAS for information about other projects.

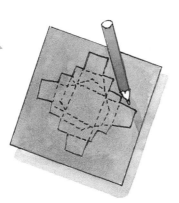

 1 Yellow squares mean this is an easy activity.

 2 Blue squares mean this is a medium activity.

 3 Pink squares mean this is a more difficult activity. You'll have to think hard!

COMPASS POINTS

For years sailors and explorers have found their way by following the points on a **compass**. The magnetic needle always points to the north so you can work out the other directions, south, west, and east. Sometimes, other points are shown in between north, south, east, and west. Halfway between north and west is — you've guessed it, north-west!

PIRATE'S TREASURE!

1 This is a good party game, you must direct the pirate to the treasure! You will need a blindfold, a big box of candy for the treasure, a large sheet of paper, and markers.

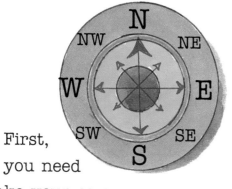

2 First, you need to make your compass. See Helpful Hints for tips on how to do this.

3 To play the game let everyone take a look at the compass. Choose a pirate and an assistant to help her. Blindfold the pirate and stand her on the compass. Spin her around but make sure she ends up facing north.

4 Hide the treasure somewhere in the room. Then the assistant must direct the pirate to the treasure. He might give directions like "turn east and take two steps forward. Now turn north-east and move four steps ..."
How long does it take to find the treasure?

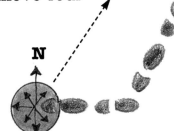

HELPFUL HINTS

● One way to remember where the different points of the compass are is to compare them to a clock face. If north is at 12 o'clock, then east is at 3 o'clock, south is at 6 o'clock, and west is at 9 o'clock.

● Another way is to make up a phrase for the letters N, E, S, and W, the initials of the main points on the compass as you move around clockwise. **N**eptune **E**ats **S**ea **W**eed is one. Can you think of another?

● You can make your own compass by folding a piece of paper into quarters. Now fold in half again to make a triangular shape like this. Unfold the paper. Now you can draw in all the compass points and decorate it to look like a real pirate's compass!

MAP REFERENCES

Finding somewhere on a map could be quite a problem, but luckily map makers make it easier for us. They draw a grid of criss-crossing lines over the map and in between each line is usually a letter or a number. Each part of the map can now be found by a reference or address.

CUP CRAZY
Can you use map references to find some candy?

1 You will need markers, a ruler, candy, cardboard, and 16 plastic cups. You could paint them so you can't see through them.

2 Draw out a grid of 16 squares on the cardboard and place a cup upside down on each square. Label the squares A, B, C, and D along the bottom and label the numbers 1, 2, 3, and 4 up the sides.

3 Secretly hide a piece of candy under one of the cups and ask your friend to guess where it is. They have to guess using a reference, for example, C2. You reply either "hot" if they have guessed correctly, "warm" if they are just one cup away, or "cold" if they are farther away.

4 How quickly can you find the candy?

HELPFUL HINTS

● It is a good habit to get used to saying the letter reference first and then the number as this is the usual way that map references are used.

MORE IDEAS

● You could play the same game but with even more cups!

● How many can you find? Make sure you ask an adult first before you borrow them for the game. They don't have to be laid out in a square — what about a rectangular grid?

● You could also play the game by hiding more than one candy; try two or three.

COORDINATES

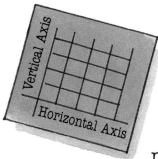

Vertical Axis

Horizontal Axis

Coordinates are used to plot points on a graph. On a flat, two-dimensional graph a pair of numbers for example (5,1) is used to show a position. The first number shows how far to move along the **horizontal axis** and the second number shows how far up the **vertical axis** the point is.

CONNECTIONS

1 Connections is a game for two players where you use coordinates to score points. You will need some cardbord, a ruler, markers, two dice, and two different sets of colored counters.

2 Make a game board like the one above. Make all the lines about 1 inch apart. Put a 0 where the lines meet then 1-6 on each axis.

(2,4)   (4,2)

3 The first player throws the two dice. If a 4 and a 2 are thrown, you can choose to place a counter on either (2,4) or (4,2).

4 Now the second player must throw the dice and place their counter in an empty position.

2 points

4 points

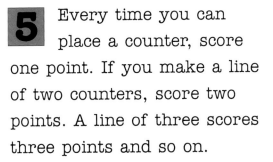

5 Every time you can place a counter, score one point. If you make a line of two counters, score two points. A line of three scores three points and so on.

6 Keep a record of your scores on a chart. The player with the highest score after 12 turns wins.

HELPFUL HINTS

● If you find it difficult to remember which coordinate comes first, you might find it helpful to think of it as "along the hall," for the first number and "up the stairs" for the second!

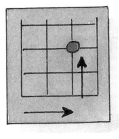

MORE IDEAS

● X Marks the Spot is a great coordinates game. You can play with the Connections grid.

● The first player secretly decides the coordinates of their hidden point, (2,2) for example, writes it on some paper, and puts it in an envelope.

● The other player guesses where it is — let's say they guess (4,4).

● Now the first player gives a clue by saying how many straight line spaces away their secret X point is. You can't count diagonal lines. In this example it is four spaces away.

● How quickly can you find where X marks the spot?

WHICH WAY?

Have you ever been lost in a maze? Mazes are full of right and left turns, and a lot of dead ends. The secret of escape is knowing which direction to take!

MINOTAUR MAZES

In Greek legend, a beast called the Minotaur lived in a maze. The maze was so complex no one ever escaped!

1 You can make your own Minotaur Mazes. You will need a large piece of plain paper, play dough, paint, and pencils.

2 Roll the play dough out into long, thin sausages. These will be the walls of your maze.

3 Place the thin rolls on the paper with some right and left turns like this.

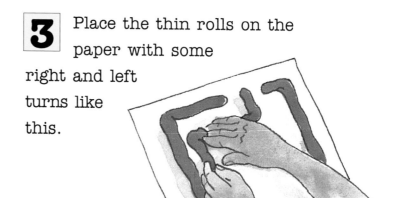

4 Make sure you leave an entrance to the maze and an exit. How difficult can you make the maze?

5 When you are happy with your maze, paint over the paper and play dough walls.

HELPFUL HINTS

● When you paint over the paper and play dough don't make the mixture too wet. It can leak under the play dough so it becomes difficult to see where the walls are.

6 Let the paint dry then remove the play dough. Draw around the edges of the walls to make them stand out clearly and challenge a friend to escape through your Minotaur Maze!

MORE IDEAS

● The Celtic people also loved mazes. Many of their designs were curved like this one.

● Can you make a maze with curves to fit inside a circle?

QUARTER TURNS

When people talk about turns they often mean a quarter turn to the left or a quarter turn to the right. A quarter turn is a little like the turn between the edges on the corner of a square.

WRAPPING PAPER PRINTS

This is a great way of using turns to make wrapping paper. You will need some large potatoes, paint, a ruler, a pencil, a knife (ask an adult first), and as big a sheet of paper as you can find.

1 Cut the potato in half like this. With a dark pencil make a design on the base of the cut potato.

2 Ask an adult to help you to use the knife to cut away the potato. Leave the design standing out.

3 On the top of the potato make a "V" shape to show the direction of your potato printing block. Now you are ready to print!

4 Choose a color and cover your block design with paint. Start at the top left of your sheet, making sure the "V" arrow is pointing directly toward you, then gently press the potato onto the sheet.

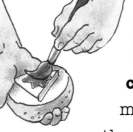

5 Now turn the potato a quarter turn **clockwise** like this and make another print in the next square.

6 Keep repeating the pattern of turns until you cover the whole sheet.

HELPFUL HINTS

● The pattern may look better if you space the prints evenly. You can make guidelines as part of the pattern by using an old ruler and a paintbrush or markers. Rest the ruler on the paper and paint or draw a line. Estimate where to put the ruler next. Be careful how you pick up the ruler, it might smear the paint on the paper!

MORE IDEAS
● You could make the pattern more interesting by using two colors.
● Why not try using different potato block designs to create more unusual patterns.

ROTATING TILES

People from many countries around the world love using tile patterns in their homes and on buildings. Some of the swirling patterns look very complicated, but are quite easy to make if you follow the pattern of turns carefully.

BLOCKS

1 You will need a block of wood about 2 inches long and 2 inches wide, scissors, a pencil, a ruler, thick string, strong glue, paint, and paper.

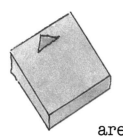

2 Mark the top of the block with an arrow so you will be able to see which way it is pointing when you are making prints.

3 On the other side make two marks on each edge of the block evenly spaced 1 inch apart.

1 in

4 Next, cut some short lengths of string and stick them on the block. Make sure that the beginning and end of the string lead from one of the marks on the block to another.

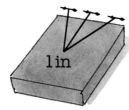

5 Cover the string in paint and press firmly onto the paper. Pick the block up carefully, **rotate** it a quarter turn clockwise, and repeat the print in the next square. Keep repeating this until the grid is full.

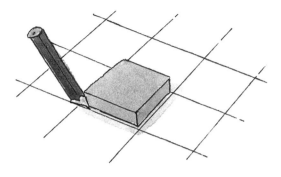

HELPFUL HINTS

● To make your block printing as accurate as possible you might find it best to begin by drawing out the square tile pattern. Using your block, trace around the outline then move the block to the first outline and keep repeating.

MORE IDEAS

● Make some more designs, but this time glue the string in straight lines from one mark to another like this. Sticking the string in straight and curved lines also produces some interesting effects. Try experimenting with different designs and different patterns of turns.

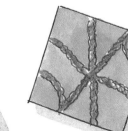

ANGLES

A quarter turn is also called a **right angle**. A square has four right angles and so does a rectangle. A right angle can be measured as having 90 **degrees**. **Angles** of less than 90 degrees are called acute. Those of more than 90 degrees are called obtuse angles.

ANGLING

1 Are you good at angling? To play this game you need to make 18 game cards. Draw angles on the back, make sure you draw six of each angle (acute, obtuse, and right). Why not draw a fish on the back? Helpful Hints gives advice on how to draw the angles.

2 The object of the game is to win as many cards as possible by collecting matching angles.

3 Shuffle the cards and lay them out flat in the "pond!" The first player turns over three cards.

4 If they are all the same type of angle, you win the cards. If they are not all the same, turn them back over, try to remember where they are, and the next player has their turn. The player with the most cards at the end wins.

HELPFUL HINTS

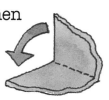

● Start by making a right-angle tester. Find a scrap of cardboard and fold it in half and half again. Make sure when you make the second fold that the folded edges meet and are straight.

● Right Angles: Draw a straight line with the ruler. Sit your tester straight on the line and then mark the right angle against the side of your tester. Mark the corner with a small square.

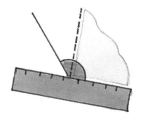

● Acute Angles:
Make sure the angle between the two lines is less than a right angle. Rest the tester on one of the straight lines. If it covers all of the angle then the angle is acute.

● Obtuse Angles: When you use the tester you will be able to see some of the obtuse angle.

MORE IDEAS
● Half a turn is 180 degrees (see page 20). Angles greater than half a turn are called reflex angles. They look bent back on themselves! Make six reflex angles and add them to the pond.

Reflex angle

DEGREES OF TURN

Do you remember that the angle between two lines can be measured in degrees. There are 360 degrees in one whole turn. Half a turn is 180 degrees and a quarter turn is 90 degrees.

WHAT'S THAT ANGLE?
How good are you at estimating angles quickly? To play this game you need to make an angle measurer.

1 Pull the arms of a compass about 2 inches apart and draw a circle on some cardboard. Draw a smaller circle about half the size inside it then cut out the large circle.

2 Choose a different color cardboard, make a circle with the compass arms at 1.5 inches apart, and cut that out, too.

3 Lightly mark the center of both circles and draw a straight line from the edge to the center of the circles. Now, cut along each line.

4 Copy the degree measurement marks around the circle you have drawn on the larger circle from this example.

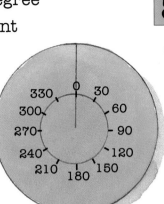

5 Slide the two circles of cardboard into each other so they overlap and the numbers are hidden. Ask your friend to find an angle. They put their finger on the angle measurer, estimating where it is.

6 Turn the smaller circle around to the finger and see if they have guessed correctly!

HELPFUL HINTS

● To mark the degrees accurately on your circle follow these steps.

● After you have drawn the smaller inside circle don't move the compass arms. Draw a cross on it. Place the compass point where the cross meets the edge of the circle and make two marks on either side of the circle (a and b).

● Repeat this on the other three points where the cross meets the circle. Draw a line from each mark through the center of the circle to the other side.

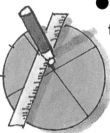

90° MORE TURNS

If you have looked at the activities on the last few pages, you will know that the angle of turn between two lines is measured in degrees. Mathematicians usually write degrees as a little circle in the air next to the number like this, 90°.

TREASURE TROVE

1 This is a great game for 2 or 3 players. Draw out the Treasure Trove grid onto some cardboard, using the hints on page 21 to help mark the angles accurately. Decorate it with bright colors.

2 Now make two sets of 20 cards. For the first set you need to mark the cards 0, 1, 2, or 3. For the second set mark the cards 0 to 9.

3 Find a treasure, like some candy, to place on each sector of the board. Now, you are ready to play!

4 The players take turns to draw one card from the first pile and two from the second. This gives a degree measurement. If it is 248° for example, they would pick up the treasure between 240° and 270°. The player who collects the most treasure wins.

30°

60°

90°

120°

HELPFUL HINTS

● If the first card you draw is a 0, it looks as if you have drawn a strange-looking number like 062°! You can ignore the 0, so the degree you have picked would be 62°.

MORE IDEAS

● You could play the same sort of game, but this time design your circle like a pizza! Cut out the 12 sectors of the circle and instead of winning the treasure in the sector you take away that part of the pizza!

MIRROR, MIRROR...

Look at your reflection in a mirror, it is exactly the same as you, except it is back to front. When a shape is reflected it might look very different or exactly the same, it depends on where you put the mirror. If it looks the same, the mirror is on a **line of symmetry.**

HALVE IT!
You might be able to draw a face, but can you draw just half?

1 Draw a straight line down the center of a piece of paper. This is your line of symmetry where you will place a mirror after you have finished drawing.

2 Draw half the face on just one side of the line.

3 It might help to fold the paper in half along the line you have drawn so you don't accidentally draw on the wrong side.

4 When you have finished your picture, put a mirror along the line of symmetry and look into it. You will see a face with two sides that are exactly the same, making a whole symmetrical face.

HELPFUL HINTS

● Before you start to draw the face, look at your own face in a mirror. Hold a large book up across half your face like this. How many eyes can you see? Ears? How much of your mouth can you see? What about your nose?

MORE IDEAS

● A famous Italian inventor and artist named Leonardo da Vinci used to keep a diary. He wanted to keep his thoughts secret so he wrote it in mirror writing, back to front! It was hard to read.

● Can you write your name in mirror writing? Try it and check by holding it up to a mirror.

REFLECTIVE SYMMETRY

Some shapes have more than one line of symmetry. This means you can put the mirror in more than one place and the shape will still look the same. A square has four lines of symmetry, a rectangle has two.

BUNTING BONANZA!

Have you ever seen bunting at a fair or a party? There are usually long lines of repeating symmetrical patterns. Often each shape in the pattern is a reflection of the one before it.

1 It is fun making these patterns — you could make one to decorate the border of a bulletin board or frame one of your pictures.

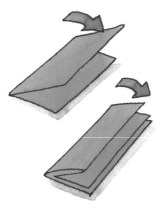

2 Fold a piece of paper in half twice like this. If you have a long piece of paper, you can make more folds.

3 With the paper still folded cut off a square from one end. Draw a shape in pencil on the paper — what about the outline of a person?

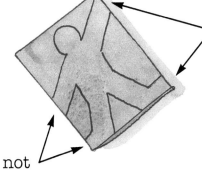

Do not cut here

Do not cut here

4 Now cut out the shape while it is still folded. Get an adult to help you with this. Don't cut the sides where the shape meets the edges. Then unfold the paper, lots of perfect mirror images of your original shape will appear!

HELPFUL HINTS

● When you draw your design, you need to make sure that it touches both sides of the square where the folds are. If you don't, when you cut out the shape all the bunting will fall into pieces!

MORE IDEAS
● This is a great way of using **reflective symmetry** to make place mats for a party. Draw around a large plate and cut it out. Fold it in half and again and once more like this. Now, use the scissors to cut out small parts. When you have finished, unfold the shape and admire your handiwork!

ROTATIONAL SYMMETRY

If a shape is moved around a central point and still looks the same when it is in its new position, we say it has **rotational symmetry**. A square has rotational symmetry of order 4 because it can be rotated four times into a different position but still appears to be the same.

IN A SPIN

You can make some amazing shapes with rotational symmetry.

 Draw a shape on some cardboard no bigger than your hand. It might have curves or straight lines or a mixture of both. Don't make it too complicated, it might be difficult to cut out!

 Cut out the shape and pierce it roughly in the middle with a push pin. You might need an adult to help you with this.

3 Put the shape in the middle of some paper and draw around it lightly. Rotate it around the push pin a quarter turn so it is facing to the right and draw around it again. Repeat this with the shape facing you then with it facing to the left.

4 Lift the shape and the push pin off the paper and use a thick marker to draw around the edge of the new shape you have created. This new shape has rotational symmetry of order 4. You will find that it can be rotated to four different positions and still look the same.

5 Cut out the shape, turn it over so you can't see the pencil lines, and stick it on a sheet of colored paper to make it look good.

HELPFUL HINTS

● When you are rotating the shape on the paper, put a thick wad of newspaper underneath, otherwise the pin might make a hole in the table!

MORE IDEAS

● It is easy to make shapes with rotational symmetry of order 8. Imagine the eight points of a compass like this.

● Make a new small shape and rotate it to face each of the eight points of the compass. Draw around the edge, or perimeter, and then cut it out and mount it as you did before.

Original shape

ANGLES AND COMPASSES

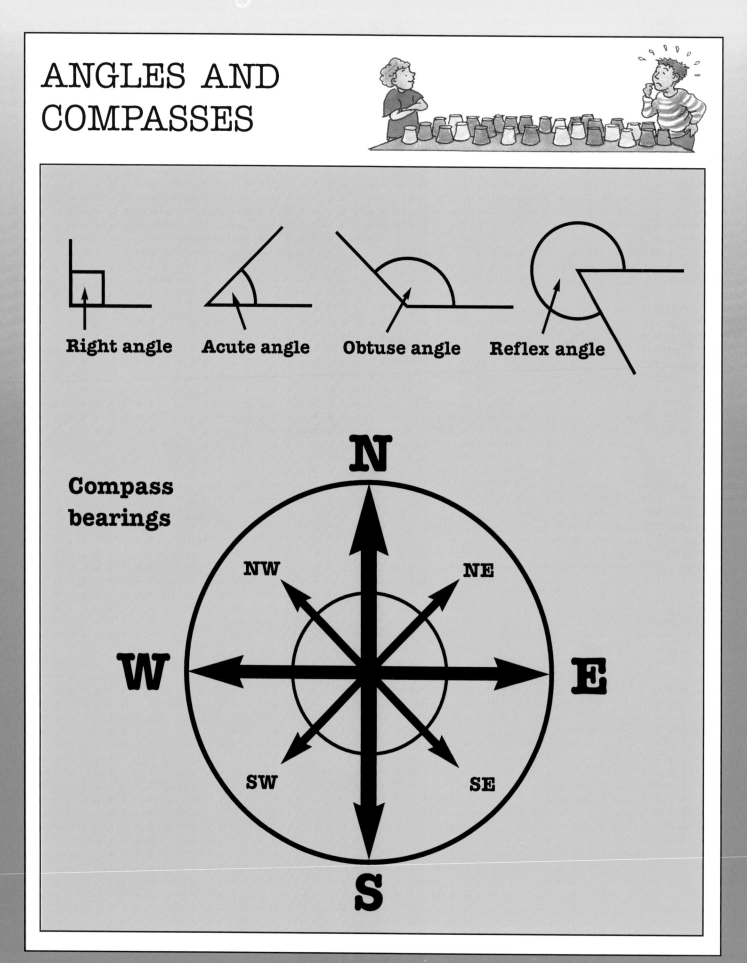

Right angle   **Acute angle**   **Obtuse angle**   **Reflex angle**

Compass bearings

N

NW   NE

W   E

SW   SE

S

GLOSSARY

Angle

An angle is the amount that something has been turned. When two straight lines cross they make an angle.

Clockwise

When you turn clockwise it means you turn in the same direction as the hands of a clock. If you turn counterclockwise, you turn in the opposite direction to the hands of a clock.

Compass

A compass helps you to find your way. It has a magnetic needle that always points north.

Coordinates

Coordinates are two numbers that show where a point is in a space, for example, on a map. The numbers (2,4) might show the position two places along and four places up a grid.

Degrees

Angles can be measured in degrees. Mathematicians use the sign ° for degrees. A full turn is 360°. A quarter turn is 90°. A half turn is 180°. A three-quarter turn is 270°.

Horizontal axis

The horizontal axis is the line going across the bottom of a graph.

Line of symmetry

A line of symmetry cuts a shape in half so that both halves look exactly the same.

Reflective symmetry

A shape has reflective symmetry if it looks the same when it is reflected in a mirror placed along a line of symmetry.

Right angle

A right angle is a quarter turn or 90°. The corners of squares and rectangles are all right angles.

Rotation

Rotation means turning around like a wheel, either to the left or the right.

Rotational symmetry

A shape has rotational symmetry if it looks exactly the same when it has been moved around a central point.

Vertical axis

The vertical axis is the line going up the side of a graph.

INDEX